3 Sages

and other poems

Poornima Dayal

India | USA | UK

Made with ❤ on the BookLeaf Publishing Platform
www.bookleafpub.in
www.bookleafpub.com

Dedication

I dedicate this book to the Almighty and to all those experiences in my life that have helped me write this book.

Preface

3 Sages is a poetry book about fantasies, experiences and learnings. As I write poetry, I realise that a lot of meaningful life lessons pour out very holistically. There's also a sense of story telling through some of these poems which may take the readers through delightful visuals and imagery.

There is reference to the divine in a lot of my poems. Pronouns starting with capital letters or written in Archaic styles usually refer to the divine.

Hope the readers enjoy these poems which I dedicate as a bunch of fragrant flowers to The Lord.

Have fun reading them.

Thanks.
Poornima Dayal

Acknowledgements

I am grateful to God. I am also thankful to my son, my husband, my mother and my loving pet as their support is invaluable.

1. Just You and me

You and me
Just us to see
with the world in Thy lap
as we clap and rap.
You make us merry
helping us ferry
across the oceans of life
without any amount of strive.
Thy resting Blue waters
with me in my halters
learning to swim
like a fish with no whims.
Just You and me
crossing the roads
holding hands, without any loads.
Faith and belief
as Ye lead my way
for I know not where I need to stay.
No horns, nor cars matter to me
not any passersby, nor any he or she

just Thy touch, a feel so secure
is all that's required for any cure.
Across imposing mountains or hills so rough
climbing is no longer tough.
Looking up at Thee is all I need
with no cares and without paying any heed.
When fires soar or flames arise
relinquishing the might of the enemies
blessing me with some prize
resting down embers and angers alike
holding me in Thy arms, making it dreamlike.
From old valleys do You keep me guarded
keeping me at bay from what's already discarded.
Just You and me,
Just You and me
with the world in Thy lap
with just no more recap.

2. Poetry

The moods of a poet, I laugh
rise and fall on a graph.
Emotions play an important role
to narrate and sing is a poet's goal.

Wordsworth, Shakespeare or Emily
narrating tales of romance, thrill and family
such brilliant poets do we read
to another world do they lead
transporting us to beauty and mysteries unknown
reading and fantasizing such have we grown.
Shakespeare's sonnets
never reveal
the speakers identity is always sealed.
Time being a frequent character,
a dark lady
coming across as sometimes shady
paradoxically repulsed or attracted to her charm
without causing himself much harm.
The fair youth, a friend of the speaker

in his earlier works did he feature,
urging him to marry and bear children
perhaps hinting at later enjoying even grandchildren.

'A solitary reaper', in school did I study
from wordsworth's poetry along with my buddy.
A famous lyrical, romantic ballad
expressing his feelings about music that are valid.
A solitary girl of great charm and beauty
comparing her tone to the Nightingale or Cuckoo
showing glimpses of what she may be upto
exploring varied realms of imagination
with strengths of seemingly unending visualization
are such poets born
boundless, intense at times forlorn.

Poetry is thy nature so pure
and fans like me does it lure
to scribble and to conjure,
of penning a few rhymes or lines am I so sure.

Robert Frost, T. S Eliot, John Keats
reading them be it cold or heat.
Enjoying, transporting me to another world
where I roam about freely without getting hurled.

3. 3 Sages

Three sages sitting under the large Bodhi tree
no families, no homes roaming around free.
Their long, Peppered beards
resembling those of great seers
their tumblers half broken
beneath the branches, lie quite shaken.

In Dharma have they found
life away from the merry go rounds
lying beneath the scorching rays-
sometimes naked,
with bodies almost half baked.
Having been to Pathshalas[1] or Gurukuls[2] in villages
having learnt sacred lessons from teachers and sages
practicing great penance now since ages.

Under nature they loom,
with musky, Sandal pastes they groom
their bodies and forehead,
without any egos which are by now dead.

Siddhata, Viddhata and Datta as names
tall and sturdy is their frame.
One holding a spiral stick
resembling somewhere a magicians trick.
Another holding his breath in deep meditation,
surrendering, rising as though in levitation.
The third a rustic, old sadhu lost in scriptures
an ancient, Archaic book without any pictures.

This land is pious, of oceans it seems
with Sunlight dropping its rays and beams.
Fruits are plenty and so are the stars
as night falls, hiding all scars.
Resting under the Bodhi tree
united in this sacred spree
to rejoice and renounce
every ounce
of worldly belongings and longings for good
away from all that since long have they stood
in penance and recitation
in devout, dutiful devotion.

Deep Red dhotis[3] and few are White
a quiet disposition is all I site.
Vermillion Tilaks[4], long marked Tripundaras[5]
of Turmeric and Sandal perhaps like Lord Indra's.

Under the Bodhi tree they sit undisturbed,
raining as it may be, still unpurturbed.
Come rain or thunder,
amidst strong winds they commit no blunder
of leaving their paths
and returning to wrath.
Free are they in spirit and mind
different from animals and other human kind.
Shiva's devotees or Krishna's messengers
traveling in their journeys as holy passengers.

Under the Bodhi tree - they sit.

---

1. School
2. House of the teacher
3. Loincloth
4. An ornamental spot worn on the forehead.
5. Three marks ,usually made with Sandal paste, a
   symbol of affiliation with Lord Shiva.

4. Lift me up

I have tried really hard
for the so called issues to ward
sometimes weary did I get
of things not getting set
working out the way I wanted
of this world was I getting daunted.

Till one day He worked upon me
bestowing new gifts is He
things and people he pleases to give
required at this moment for me to live.
A happy and blessed life,
fluid and without any strive
His special blessings from his treasury so sublime
for me to cherish from time to time.

As I cried from within, letting out a loud cry
hard and long did I try
cajoling me thus, in His arms so loving
all those miseries is He shoving

under the sand
beneath the land
asking me to hold His hands.
No means in sight, or may be somewhere a tiny chance
for things to work out I may get some glance.
At times giving up though at times letting go in belief
such desires does the heart hold for some weird reliefs.
Expectations they say serve no purpose
be happy and don't make a circus
living in acceptance of what comes our way
is surely the way to live, enjoy and play.
Oh God, what is human existence
why is there so much persistence
for things that may not be working out
why does the heart scream or shout?.

Contentment, a virtue to possess
ain't always that easy a process
for immense faith and love are required
to let go of all that I may have ever enquired.

Gazing at His surreal form
is the only way to transform,
to beg pardon and conform
without any worries of how I may perform.

Oh Lord, lift me to Thy joyful state

You are mighty and oh so great
and I know it's just never too late
allowing undoubtable trust to reinstate.

5. Badminton

It was a day of jubilation
a day of absolute celebration
when two hearts met
across the badminton net
when eyes crossed and glances exchanged
a meeting so divinely prearranged.

He is John and she is Miah
playing doubles next with Jack and Tiah.
His hair a curly, Whisky Brown
wearing a Purple cap on his crown.
Sporty, dashing and so lean
to play his sport, he is keen.
Miah, her long, flowing hair
playing her sport with John as a pair.
Today is their game, a match at national levels
against tough opponents as their rivals.
In Red shorts and sneakers
while the commentator shouts on speakers
announcing the scores and their every move

with music playing at a distant where children groove.

Amidst Orange trees and Apple orchards,
on Green, lush lawns
moving swiftly like Chess pawns.
The Sun shone bright
it's long before night,
oh such a fun filled, joyful sight.

Wiping sweat off their Rosy faces
tieing again those opened shoe laces
as John jumps, then ducks a little
as Jack hits the shuttle to far off places.

Miah jumping with all her might,
her bosoms leaping from left to right.
Those salty eyes
and excited cries,
waving her Silvery racket,
wearing a dark jacket.

From far and wide they come,
girls, boys and their favorite chums
to witness this match
as the Sunlight does the badminton net doth catch.
Sounds of loud cheering
for the next shot are the players gearing

a game so swift
sometimes low, at times a lift.

Back and forth as it flies
soaring high, almost touching the Blue skies
like a bird in paradise,
playing with commitment they do, as passions arise.
Hanging between those tall posts
the net and the game of shuttle that the country club
hosts.
Floating in the air, dropping from above
hitting it hard, it's Thirteen love.
Tiah dashes and covers some lost game points,
hastily and eagerly, almost bruising her knee joints.
Victory means the world to her
as of now its like a blur.
Jack was good but not now she thinks
brushing off her sweat as she blinks.
What went wrong, a despairing Jack wonders
where did he make all such blunders
gripping still with his fists so tight,
avoiding an argument or any fight
portraying still a sense of delight.

It's his last serve and John's ready to begin
wishing so much that they would win.
Hurrah! Its a game point and they have won

and for the audiences its been so much fun.

John and Miah, together do they roll
on warm grasses where people usually stroll.
A couple are they, so brave and bold
a victory cup in their hands they triumphantly hold.

6. Transient

Not believing in living on memories
nor retaining any sort of diaries
happy ones may be relished for moments
thanking the Lord for His bestowments.
Its all transient and temporary
not even a shadow for us to marry
it may be about Tom, Julie or Harry.

Divinity being the only forever
for us to serve and rever.
My aunts or uncles were oh so good
not living in their constant thoughts is what I
understood.
No life is ever eternal
human flesh and bones are just externals.

Yes, flashing, happy thoughts I rejoice
some from my past or of my choice.
Few fleeting reminiscents
of times flown by

there's nothing more to think and cry
just remembering to forever bid good bye.
It may sound crude
or immensely rude
but it ain't really uncouth
to be living in truth.

My father's death led me on
to learn such lessons, bringing it on
to pray and serve every night till dawn.
Trusting His mighty show
for us to learn, live and finally go.
Making new friends or relations,
learning to cope with such situations,
living with Him as we are all His creations.
No lasting impacts did ever serve
there's no point in illtreating our mind or any nerve
by crying, missing or living in grief
learning this has been such a relief.
In Gratitude I spread my arms
bowing, admiring His Holy charm.
Its only Him in life or death
in every bit, in every breath.
Be it living subjects
or every non living object,
be it the so called lost possessions
seeking for which are humans sessions

no worth nor value must we attach
learning to always love and detach.

I am but a passer by
transient and momentary
born to live, unlearn and make merry.
A gift is life of supreme order
to pray and learn should be our primary fodder .
I am just a passer by
worshiping Him is all I wish to do or atleast try.

7. The Turkish fair

The Clarinet, I whispered
it's a glistening Gold and Red.
A Soprano or a Sopranino,
walking to the fair am I with my friend Lino.

Holding and playing is this man from Turkey
enthralling all, its so quirky.
This merry Turkish fair
with girls wearing dresses in layers,
with merry go rounds and rides so rare.

A Cobalt Blue armour resting on a string
for sale it is, belonging to an old king.
Nice looking girls are ready to sing
with them bags and shawls to they bring.
Fancy costume dresses for sale,
Ceramic and Glass paintings hanging on nails,
Woolen Rugs
and Porcelain mugs,
Handcrafted pottery, textiles and carpets

all these goods selling at small markets
or bazars may be as they are called
within the fair, from all sides it's walled.

Delectable kebabs, Manti and Simit
of such delicious dishes there is no limit.
Juicy meats
are such a treat
coming to this fair do we relish and eat.
Such incredible hospitality is never before seen
for serving us with love they are so keen.
Such piping hot, cardamom Kahwa
we couldn't have ever tasted in Sumatra or Jawa.

And we see these Armenian folk dancers,
they are obviously free lancers,
dancing to loud pipes and drums
walking towards them are we, as we mildly hum.
Men wearing traditional head dresses
and jackets well pressed,
with girls in colorful, long dresses
with well combed tresses.
'Gna - Gna', as they sing
wearing ornaments of Silver and bling
a famous folk song
to Armenia does it belong.

I see a crowd gathering, its an oil wrestling match
queuing are people so that a glimpse they may catch.
With oiled bodies and muscled arms
watching them wrestle am I charmed.
Holding steadfast on to the grounds
gripping, rooted to the land
as they fight on White, slippery sands.
A game of tactics more than strength
stretched across the fields breadth and length.
My hero wins, Brown in body
with clear, Blue eyes and nothing about him is shoddy.

Charming Horse riders walking with stride
holding their reins are they tight.
Wearing high-healed, polished, leather boots
dressed in shimmery hats and cowboy suits.
From far off markets have they come
listening as they do the pipe and drum.

Liking a piece of ancient, stone pendant
of Marble with engravings, looking resplendent.
Picking it up and trying it on
with a thread like chain in Cream and Fawn.
Such fun it is to visit this fair
and to pen now and to share
all such memories that are so prime
while pecking on an Olive cake with Pepper and Thyme.

8. Hear me Lord

Don't know from where this cry is coming
too loud, from somewhere within blaring
to be told, to be heard
by Ye, my Lord Jesus, the holy shepherd.

What's this stringing
sometimes alarming
know I that its not harming
my heart or my very veins
causing no loss nor any gains.
Memories of the past or are they incidents
or missing someone, I know it can't be redundant.
Is it a lover's cry, a devotee seeking a place to try
at His Holy feet so pure
where I belong and I am sure.

Pulling, tugging - oh, don't be so loud
I will definitely act upon to get you out of this cloud.
No tears are seen
they remain unseen

a feeling of not being well
at times it swells.
Oh Jesus, just hug me tight
not asking for pity on such a plight
but bathe me now in Thy Love
with sparkling lights and strength from above.
Rub on me Thy healing touch
that eternal balm, I thank Ye so much.

Mellowing now as I hear
that noise or cry that I did share.
Calling, writing to Ye my childlike words
pray I surrender to You all and not just one thirds.

Hear me Lord, at times I scream
is it some wierd sadness or some steam?.
Whatever it be, just hold me now
as I bend and appeal, before saying ciao.

9. Travel

The most incredible journeys of my life
where there may have been many a husbands and
wives.
Such amazing travels within dreams or visions
to sacred lands, of God's and decisions.
No boundaries, no limits do they need
no deadlines ever to complete.
A passing journey like short destinations
or a lengthy dream with divine visitations.
A romantic saga
or a television drama,
a playing reel
and perhaps I kneel.
Of passions and mermaids,
of brides or bridesmaids,
of mysterious men
seeking me in their den,
of waves in the water,
at the wheel, I am with the potter.
Such varied visions

they may be fictions,
playing at the piano, perhaps
without too many gaps.

Such fancy travels
and journeys they be
sometimes once or multiple repeats
closing my eyes and as my heart beats.
Visions may be clear
and from somewhere people jeer,
may be past memories
resembling harsh queries.
Love does happen, in sublime ways
or romance is it as my heart does graze
to pastures unknown
in this dream like zone
in journeys are written such fascinating parables,
such splendid and delightful fables.
My heart does speak as the mind rests
of narratives, descriptives - such celebratory fests.

Such joys from the creator
there ain't no predator
in a space of our own
where we don't feel alone.
These travels are frequent
where we are eloquent

of pictures and stories are they made
flowing incessantly cause they are supremely laid.
Involving no expense, no costs at all
its fun and frolic, its just free for all.

10. Regal Love

A highly accomplished dancer was she
before British times when there used to be
some respect and dignity
when there was assurance and guarantee.
Zahara, as she was famously called
there isn't much history about her to recall
a pretty, dark lady with features so sharp
forever singing songs on her Aeolian Harp.
Wearing her pleated, Rust skirt
wrapped around her slim girth
with tiny mirrors was it bedecked
when her lover on her checked.
Courtesan of a wealthy man
an imperial, august king with a light Brown tan.

Knotting around his lady love
rapturously listening to those songs about Doves.
Pleading she never leaves
embracing him warmly as she heaves
the harp on a wooden, old trunk

while her man is slightly drunk.
Noble was their affection
with no need for any correction.
By her beauty and charm was he smitten
removing from his arms those long White mittens.
A play of romance, some laughter and mischief
humming along notes of a lovers trail,
hoping to mount a boat about to set sail.

A connection was made between her music and dance
wrapping himself around her, was he left in a trance.
Her emotional expressions had her revealing,
her gestures so passionate, could not have him leaving.
Fondling her twisted hair,
and such deep love did they share
begging to be left as she did in those impish voice notes
holding her face with devotion as he would dote.
A graceful swan dance,
an elegant stance
moving those dainty arms,
letting out her wide palms.

Glimmering Moonlight shone so brightly,
reflecting it's glow across the waters so rightly.
Some enchanting trees whispering a spellbinding chant,
an amorous feeling do they grant,
swaying to and fro

as the lovers go
into their chambers
with burning fires like glowing Ambers.

Musicians may be heard at a distance
as the Harmonica they play,
swiftly melting into the night as clay.
When birds are asleep and so are their consorts,
when Peahen rest
close to the bird's nest.

Such intimacy and fondness may never again be seen
in times more modern that they had forseen.
Her body slowly wriggles
as his hands gently snuggle,
clasping those rounded bosoms
as his fists he carelessly loosens,
touching her tender lips,
moving her ample hips...

11. The Bard of Kyrgyzstan

Singing celebratory songs of achievements
as they defended their country on all fronts
the Kyrgyz, at their best
not one bit will they rest
fighting the enemies
bending on their knees....
such lores did he play on his favorite stringed Lute
just before putting aside his melodious Flute.
The bard of Kyrgyztan
a short, burly man of freckled, White skin,
his Gold fish in the pond flapping its bright finn...

As he sits in his dim lit room reminiscing past glories,
contuining to be that flamboyant and charismatic
telling tales from history that are no longer enigmatic
Now in his fifties,
once earning a good fees.
Clad in a light armour
oh, what a charmer ....is he!

'Salamatsyzby - Salamatsyzby',
come forth some children
from nearby homes, roasted Fish and Meats do the
bring....
Singing songs from yore
as his Black, old shoes they adore.
Admiring the shine, feeling the armour
sliding, gliding their fingers,
rubbing the steel, and some near by Timbers...

The bards music is to listen
of soldiers and men in prison
of wars, victories or treason
across cold winters or summer seasons....
Dancing, vacillating, stopping and hearing,
running, rolling, smiling or elated,
are children playing with his Velvety robes and Tan hats
elongated.

The bard of Kyrgyztan,
magic in his instruments
those lengthy, slim fingers as they cajole
playing their oh so significant role.
Dressing up his Lute
in a Golden bag of jute

taking off to serenade
walking towards a marching, army parade...

12. A poem for my son

One radiant, Sunny afternoon,
a young, White stork flew over my nest,
while I was napping and taking some rest
with you in its arms oh, my bundle of joy,
handing over my precious little gift from God - ahoy.

You made me feel whole,
you complimented my soul,
it was celebration time,
I did a jig or two and rock and roll.

Your calm and glittering eyes,
stared at me in awe,
admiring the woman,
in me your mom you saw.

As days rolled to months and years,
I saw you play and study without fears.
Now with you so grown up,
filling as you do your coffee cup,

I grip your hands lovingly and warmly,
thanking you for choosing me so strongly.

Oh, my knight in shinning armour,
my caring, bright charmer,
blessed with immense love from the Gods
having won so many accolades and rewards,
know that I will always stand besides
be it on plains, plateaus or even through landslides.

Thanking the Lord for my handsome child
and sometimes when I called and dialed
when he was in far away lands,
while combing by hair in curly strands
calling him back as I had waited
in my country home with walls so gated.

Returning to me, am I overjoyed
filling my heart and that past void.
Standing by you every night and day
hoping the Lord keeps me alive and gay.

13. Reverence

From the depths of my heart,
from within the joys of living,
there's a whisper, albeit sometimes a roar,
ready to be heard
told aloud
spoken and expressed.

Tears of unspoken words and joy
come pouring down
sometimes on canvas or on paper.
Reds, Blues, Crimson and Pristine Whites,
as new chapters unfold
one story leading to another,
I bow in Gratitude
for what may have been, for what is and
for what will be.

Remaining untarnished, nourished
in the rays of Thy Love,
I surrender and bow,

as the artist in me unfurls,
yet another story of contentment,
joy, learning and gratitude.

14. To art with love

When people ask me my favourite art,
is it 'Tokyo', 'The Script' or the one with a hidden heart?.
I laugh and smile from within
just how may I compare, the lines so thin.
Of colors are my art pieces
fawned over by my nephews and nieces.

Art is a state of the mind
always helping us remind
our life and our very existence
expressing them as I do with consistence.
Reflecting my very being
my emotions as I am seeing
some of unknown joys
or clandestine affairs
presented as abstracts at well known art fairs.
It may be dripping a tear or more
in Black's or hues, with sentiments so pure.
Like watery eyes,
using colorful dyes

Inks, Pastels, Oils and Acrylics
and my heart and mind may even frolic.

A cascading line like a spiraled rope
trying to unknot, reviving hope.
A giant hillock or homes with slopes,
a man and women trying to elope.
Varied themes with concepts and textures
its not about halting or juggling with fixtures.

Fascinated by different styles
I may even travel at times a few miles
to see more art or learn from them,
theres always scope to stich the hem.

I am just a novice, though years its been
and some say its in my gene.
A student or disciple perhaps
painting in revered holy laps
guided as I may be,
allowing me to be mentally free.

Thanking my art to let me be
and helping me forever see
the marvels of Fire, Earth, the skies and the seas.
A rush in my blood to hold the brush
may be love, my stable crush..

15. Standing undivided

Speaking are some of a society of classes
but even if I were to see through my special glasses
not much can I find, any difference or divide
just no demarcation that may be so wide.

They say they are high class
and its such rich, Green grass
they may be owners of mills,
holding their wine glasses tall and still
driving the Rolls Royace or Ferrari perhaps
with jewels and so called luxuries dropping in their laps.
Show me humility and I will rise
regarding them capable and calling them wise.

Laughing at the meek, for they are called week
mistaking identities is a common human streak.
Being shy, quiet or reserved
may be regarded as being absurd.
Mocking them loud
may be a crowd,

cheering and rewarding such
may be just a few of us.
Being a part of this coy lot
was I of some sorts.
In my past, in days of my youth
when people considered it to be my truth
not a whisper did I make nor leaf I shake
knowing well enough there was just nothing at stake
to proove or show
how far I could go.
Just be led by Him
without whom I can just never swim
in this world or across the oceans,
when still or in motion,
through life or its strides
on the slow and fast rides,
there is just no divide....
between the silent or the loud,
between the so called poor or the proud.

16. The murmurs of Nature

Offering my gratitude to Mother Nature's glory
with symphony reverberating through her sounds and
every story.
Dancing across wide rivers are Red, striped Mullets
whispering their voice notes in these tiny rivulets,
meandering their way through flooded streams
as bees buzz over the budding floral screens.

Did you hear the voice of the dark?
enchanting, eluding yet vociferously stark.
There flows the stream, merging with the cascading
waterfall,
Green, croaking Frogs - running or are they trying to
crawl?.
English Sparrows making their nests
or bright, colourful Parrots flying from East to West.
Was there a descent of Woodpeckers diving into festive
woods
carrying with them nuts, seeds and insects, as many as
they could.

Monkeys are swinging from branch to branch
staying away from Eagles, they aren't taking any chance.
The notably sweet Birch tree,
providing shelter to wildlife all for free.

Gushing are some distant waters,
telling me such tales from all quarters,
a murmur can thus be heard
hoping by now the moods are spurred.

~

17. The train from Amritsar to Lahore

Rail Rail come again
helping us once more regain.
Across the borders,
looking at all corners
moving from Amritsar to Lahore
never have they been before.
A bunch of four,
and some seated on the floor,
some occupying high berths
from origins so diverse.

Playing a game of friendly Rummy,
children running to be with their mummy,
lifting bags, heavy or light
its surely in the mid of night.
Eager to meet their old relatives at a distance
hoping to offer them their assistance,
or perhaps moving to lands
where their hearts did once stand.

Turbaned, in crisp cotton shirts,
few clean shaven, reminiscing their births.
Polka dotted suit she wears,
below shawls and sweaters clad, in layers.
That four year old boy is loudly yelling
to his dad to hear a story compelling.

Outside they see the Wagah border
while traveling in their train, in the right order.
Soldiers from the national army marching
their beloved lands are they guarding.
In Khaki, Green and Olive dresses,
living in Army tents or protected, government addresses.
With bushy moustaches and well combed beards
participating in the parade, are they cheered.

Crackling sounds of colored Glass bangles
putting her child to sleep as she handles
perched on a side berth
with her is another child so full of mirth
playing Ludo is he
with his friend and partner Balli.
'Chai- Chai ' sounds of a tea vendor
selling piping hot tea and Samosas, male is he in gender.
A money bag wrapped around his slim waist
appears to be making haste,

moving from one cabin to another
rushing with speed as passengers wonder.

Kulwinder, this pretty daughter of Satwinder
dressed in Black and striped Yellow
going to meet her brother, some good fellow.
Singing melodious songs from Bollywood
mixing lyrics with words from Pollywood.

A misty night can be seen,
outside as the sky is lit by the Moon beams.
Smells of peppered Grams and Peanuts roasted
stalls lining across the station, selling breads with jam
toasted.
Morning is approaching soon
a while before it may be noon.

Some having started their Journey from Delhi
till Amritsar did they ferry
enjoying with friends and making merry.
On way to Lahore, while halting at Amritsar in Punjab
and some women were even dressed in their cosy hijab.
A train that was from Amritsar to Lahore
telling tales are we from the lore,
the Samjhauta Express as it was called
since years has now it been stalled.

18. The Tiger of Tadoba

The tiger of Tadoba
a favorite with Vinoba
those impish eyes, twinkling under a strong Sunrise
with pots of water at the reserve daily does he arrive.
For my 'Sakha', as he adoringly calls
his majestic friend, within an area with rough walls,
holding hands of Kacha, the caretaker,
feeding Water and Rice is their Icebreaker.
A daily routine,
before they eat their Greens
to feed him with some Meats so clean
slurping and rolling his tongue
does he proceed,
thanking the boy for his good deed.

Such bonds are rarely ever seen
between man and his friend 'Sakha', oh, what a scene
A friendly tiger is he
with eyes so sharp that they could see.
No enemy nor huntsman,

no villains in this piece
just him and Vinoba
a bond that can never cease.
His big, White belly with spotted ears
to Vinoba an everlasting friend is he so dear.
Such timeless love has never been seen
gaping at this are visitors with looks really keen.

Bathing his stripes
as Vinoba wipes
his dainty fingers,
on his soft coat linger
patting and dressing him up like a king
affectionately always do they cling.
A Six month old cub
sipping water from his tub
under the mighty Sun rays
as Vinoba makes way.

To the reserves of Tadoba - Andhari
coming from villages are also Akriti and Pandhari,
a devotee of Pandharpur
bringing his friend to Chandrapur
visiting this National Park as they do
trying earnestly is he to woo
her hands in marriage
without any carriage

watching the tigers is her passion
simple and devout is she, with no fondness for fashion.
Those large, black eyes
smiling under those dusky skies,
as evening approaches
and they rush before it closes.

The tiger of Tadoba
waiting for his friend Vinoba
today's another day
theres so much new he wants to say.

Jumping, skipping there he comes
as a folklore he hums ..

19. Concert

Watching and listening to an endearing concert.
Did it lead me to paths then unknown
of love, fame, pleasure and exultation.

Caring for self, dancing to drums
moving briskly to the Electric guitar.
What a super guitarist,
strumming as though there were no end
his fingers warmly seducing.
his Purple guitar.

The singer, a White, American man
about 60 odd years old
with his voice of Gold.
A handsome face with high cheek bones,
a slim, sturdy body
wearing high-heeled, Black shoes.

Under those heavy Fog lights
his Royal Blue Shirt,

lacy ,glossy and ever appealing.
With hair, straight and well combed
A Pruny, Blackish-Brown.

'Everything I do...' as he hums
the crowds cheering thunderously.
Plenty clapping hands, others shaking and rejoicing,
grooving to his mellifluous voice
admiring his gut and nerves.
Loud can it be heard,
till a distance - till a distance!

As I sway, along the beats
little do I know what I ever did
to deserve such fantabulous treats.

Wooing, winning so many hearts
with some lovers holding hands
or waltzing with stupendous zing.
Several arms around their women's waists ,
do many men whirl and twirl around.

Considering myself the chosen one
for night another could not have been.
Oh, such melody, you earn my heart.
This awesome, splendid, supreme bliss.

20. Lead me on

My prayer to Ye oh Lord so great
is to lift me above fear and all such traits.
To remove sundry shadows
as You be the only one who knows
of all my highs and lows.

Lift me up under Thy blissful mercies
keeping me away from controversies.
Lift me up to Thy light and shine
where I may not have to pay any fine
to people unknown or even known
to events or situations that life may ever have thrown.
They are but passing phases
not even worth writing in phrases.
Fill me with Thy perennial light
dressing me up like a bright Knight.

Circambulating around the holy fires
worshiping and asking for my desires
to be fulfilled by Thy grace

keeping me forever in Your embrace.
I am but a molecule, an atom or may be even less,
non existent perhaps,
in Thy presence we rest our caps.

Tranquility do I seek
humming, singing from my cheek to cheek
songs in praise
do I raise
for Thy blessings
as Ye be caressing
my life, my hands, my very heart
filling Thy love in my cart.

Praise be to You oh my Messaiah
oh my Lord and my holy Gaia.
For creating this land and people like us
for creating animals and water bodies thus.
For guiding, leading me on Thy path
delivering me, shielding me Thou Hath.

Lead me on...Lead me on.

21. Don't give up

Never give up
it may not be showing up,
don't let the spirit fail
come rain or hail.
Keep working
keep moving
trying every corner
theres nothing in this of any dishonor
in being ourselves
in doing for yourself.

They may be quiet or irresponsive
its not the end, seek others who may be responsive
not a game of chance or dice
no loss nor victory, it's not a vice.
Don't give up darlings
there may be some good,
sometimes, somethings we haven't yet understood.
Putting in efforts
or may be a word

doing are best always, ain't absurd.

Rumours may be many
don't give it a penny,
walking straight and tall
this may be our call.
Gossiping is an art
we must not play it's part,
heading as we do
towards what's required of me and you.

Don't give up, we must look above
the knight is with us, always giving us love.
There's always a place
for every Queen or Ace
theres just no need to be in any race.
Its your's if its meant
theres nothing to lament
just give it our best
and leave the rest
as His hands do bless
it's not a game of chess.
Surrendering and rendering
love to ourselves
theres no better ways to spend on ourselves.

Don't give up, just let time pass

its written above, its not burnt grass.
Look at the harvest and marvel thus
nothing to cry or even to fuss.

Don't give up darlings, for its true
its meant to happen, its just for you.